USING MATHS

FIREFIGHTERS
To THE RESCUE

Wendy Clemson and David Clemson

Copyright © ticktock Entertainment Ltd 2007
First published in Great Britain in 2007 by ticktock Media Ltd.,
Unit 2, Orchard Business Centre, North Farm Road,
Tunbridge Wells, Kent, TN2 3XF

ticktock project editor: Rebecca Clunes
ticktock project designer: Sara Greasley

ISBN 978 1 84696 061 1
Printed in China
A CIP catalogue record for this book is available from the British Library.

Picture credits
t=top, b=bottom, c=centre, l-left, r=right
Peter Casolino/Alamy 10; Comstock Images/Alamy 30; FEMA/ Andrea Booher14-15; FEMA/ Justin Domeroski 16;
FEMA/ Bob McMillan 17; Shutterstock 1, 2, 3 (all), 4 (all), 5, 6-7, 8, 9, 12-13, 18-19, 20, 21, 22T, 22B, 23, 24,
26T, 26B, 27, 28, 29, 31T, 31B, 32; Jiang Jin/SuperStock 25
Cover: all Shutterstock except main image front cover by Flying Colours Ltd/ Getty

Every effort has been made to trace the copyright holders, and we apologise in advance for any unintentional omissions.
We would be pleased to insert the appropriate acknowledgements in any subsequent edition of this publication.

Contents

Welcome to the Fire Station

You are a firefighter at a busy fire station. You help to put out fires and rescue people in trouble. Your job is dangerous but it makes you feel good to help other people. Your skills and bravery save lives.

What does a firefighter do?

Most of the fires you put out are in homes, shops and offices.

You also have to put out fires in the countryside.

You tell people how fires start and what they can do to stop them.

Sometimes you talk to children about your job.

But did you know that firefighters sometimes have to use maths?

In this book you will find lots of number puzzles that firefighters have to solve every day. You will also get the chance to answer lots of number questions about fires, firefighters and fire safety.

What's inside the book?

Find out what needs to be done next in your busy day.

Answer the questions and practise your maths skills.

The charts and tables will help you answer the maths questions.

Look out for facts about being a firefighter!

How Fast Can They Go?

The fire engine races through the traffic. The lights flash and the siren is making a loud noise. The lights and siren tells other drivers to pull out of the way so you can get past.

This is the traffic in one lane of a main road.

1. How many vehicles need to pull over to let the fire engine through?

2. The fire engine can go about 2 kilometres in 3 minutes. How far can it go in 6 minutes?

3. The lights flash 60 times in one minute. How many times do the lights flash in 1½ minutes?

Drivers are specially trained to drive safely at high speeds.

FIRE-RESCUE

8

Here is a diagram. It is made of 16 squares.

4. What do you find at number 13 on the diagram?

5. What is at number 3 on the diagram?

6. What number is the house on?

7. What is to the left of the 7 on the map?

1	2		4
5		7	8
9	10	11	
	14	15	16

KEY
tree
camp fire
fire engine
house

9

If you get stuck, there are some tips to help you on pages 30-31.

Are you ready to be a firefighter for the day?

You will need paper, a pencil, a ruler and don't forget to wear your firefighter's uniform! Let's go...

Your Fire Station

You are a firefighter in one of your town's fire stations. You could be called out to a fire at any time. You deal with all sorts of fires. Fires don't just happen in people's homes – there are plenty of fires in the countryside too.

Here are the numbers of workers at a station.

2 fire chiefs – they decide how fire should be put out

2 crew leaders – they organise the firefighters

12 firefighters – they tackle the blaze

1 If these workers are in two equal teams, how many people are there in each team?

2 Your station is always busy! Last year you put out 130 big fires and 100 small fires. How many more big fires than small fires?

3 Your team put out 60 car fires and 15 house fires. What is the total number of car and house fires?

WHERE IS THE FIRE?

This graph shows the number of fires last month.

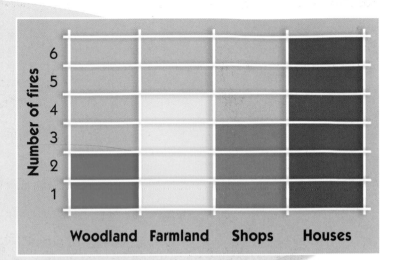

4 How many fires on farmland were there?

5 How many fires altogether?

Most fire stations have at least two fire engines.

Starting Your Shift

When you arrive at work there are always lots of things to do, even when there are no fires. You have to make sure that everything on the fire engine works well. You keep the fire station clean and tidy.

Firefighters are needed night and day. They work in shifts. A 'shift' is the time that a firefighter spends at work. It can be a 'day' shift or a 'night' shift.

1 This week you will work four day shifts. How many days in the week are you not working a day shift?

2 The clock shows the time in the morning when you start work. What time is it?

YESTERDAY'S TIMETABLE

You were not called out to a fire yesterday. Here is what you did instead.

9:00 to 10:30	Checked the engine
10:30 to 11:00	Break
11:00 to 12:00	Training
12:00 to 1:00	Cleaning
1:00 to 2:00	Lunch

3 What were you doing at 10:00?

4 What were you doing at 11:30?

5 What were you doing at 1:15?

6 After lunch, you spent another hour cleaning. You then showed a group of children around the fire station until it was time to go home. You finished work at 5:00 pm. How long did the visit from the children last?

NEW CLOTHES

Today you are getting a new uniform! The storeroom has lots of hats, trousers and jackets. You choose the clothes that fit you the best.

7 What is the difference between the numbers of helmets and jackets in the storeroom?

8 What is the difference between the numbers of trousers and jackets?

14 helmets

36 trousers

18 jackets

Uniforms protect firefighters from the heat. They are also waterproof!

The Alarm Call

Someone has dialled 999. There is a fire in the town! The alarm bell at the fire station rings. All of the firefighters jump up and rush to the fire engine. It takes just 60 seconds for you to leave the station. You are on your way!

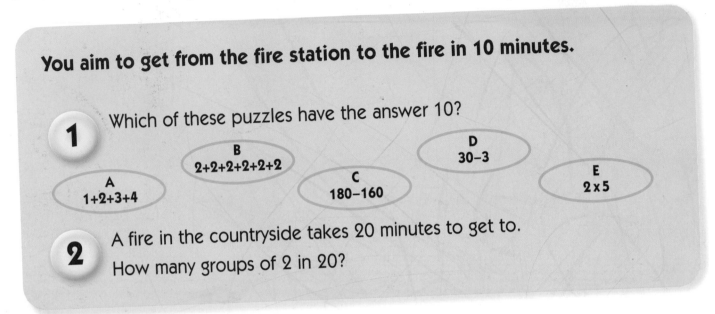

You aim to get from the fire station to the fire in 10 minutes.

1 Which of these puzzles have the answer 10?

A
1+2+3+4

B
2+2+2+2+2+2

C
180−160

D
30−3

E
2 × 5

2 A fire in the countryside takes 20 minutes to get to. How many groups of 2 in 20?

Specially trained operators take 999 calls. They find out details of the emergency and then let the fire station know.

3 The alarm bell sounds. It takes the firefighters one minute to get to the fire engine and leave the station. It then takes two minutes for them to reach the main road and three minutes for them to arrive at the fire. How long has it been since the alarm bell rang?

WHERE IS THE FIRE?

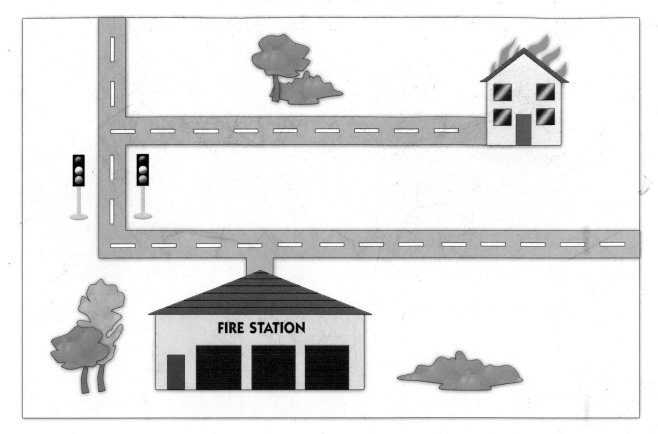

4 Look at the map of your town. You need to give the driver directions. Would you choose A, B or C?

A Turn left out of the station, then left again, go past the traffic lights and then right

B Turn right out of the station, then left, go past the traffic lights and then turn left

C Turn left out of the station, then right, go past the traffic lights and then turn right

How Fast Can They Go?

The fire engine races through the traffic. The lights flash and the siren is making a loud noise. The lights and siren tells other drivers to pull out of the way so you can get past.

This is the traffic in one lane of a main road.

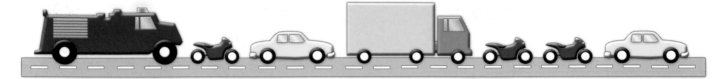

1 How many vehicles need to pull over to let the fire engine through?

2 The fire engine can go about 2 kilometres in 3 minutes. How far can it go in 6 minutes?

3 The lights flash 60 times in one minute. How many times do the lights flash in 1½ minutes?

Drivers are specially trained to drive safely at high speeds.

Here is a diagram. It is made of 16 squares.

1	2		4
5		7	8
9	10	11	
	14	15	16

(4) What do you find at number 13 on the diagram?

(5) What is at number 3 on the diagram?

(6) What number is the house on?

(7) What is to the left of the 7 on the map?

KEY

 tree

camp fire

fire engine

 house

Forest Fire

There is a fire in the woods. In hot, dry weather, there is a big risk of fires. The dry wood and leaves mean there is lots of fuel for the fire. A strong wind can make a forest fire spread very quickly.

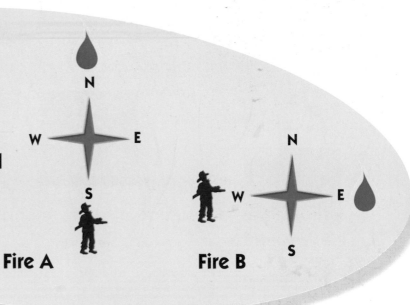

Firefighters check the direction of the wind. It is very dangerous to be in front of the fire if the wind is pushing it towards you.

Fire A

Fire B

1 Look at Fire A. The wind is blowing from North to South. Is the firefighter safe?

2 At Fire B, the wind is blowing from West to East. Is the firefighter safe?

A big wildfire can burn about 2 square kilometres in an hour.

14

A FIRE PICTOGRAM

Firefighters look for clues to work out how the fire started. Here is a pictogram showing how forest fires started last year.

How the fire started	Number of fires
Lightning strike	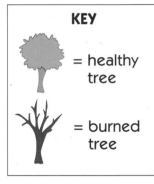
Camp fire	
Deliberately started	

= one fire

3 How were most fires started?

4 How many fires were there altogether?

5 Some trees die after a forest fire, but others can recover and have new leaves in the spring. How many of these trees are burned?

KEY

= healthy tree

= burned tree

The fire engine has all of the equipment you will need to tackle this forest fire. It carries long hoses and different sorts of ladders as well as 1800 litres of water. The fire engine also has powerful lights to help the firefighters when they work in the dark.

The fire engine's ladders are 13½ metres long and 10½ metres long.

1 How much higher can the longer ladder reach?

You can see the first eight rungs of this ladder.

2 You are standing on rung 4 and move down 2 steps. What rung are you standing on now?

3 You are on rung 3 and climbs up 5 steps. What rung are you on now?

Firefighters make sure a fire is completely out in one area before moving on to the next.

16

The engine can pump about 40 litres of water in one second.

Fire engines can carry about 1 kilometre of hose.

4 How much water does it pump in three seconds?

THE WATER TRUCK

As well as engines, the fire station also has a water truck. It can carry over 9000 litres! That is much more water than the engine can carry.

5 Fire engines have two hoses. Water trucks have five. How many hoses on two fire engines and one water truck?

The forest fire is out, but the station radios you. There is a fire in town – can you go straight there?

Rescue Mission

Time for your next call! You have arrived at the house fire. Before you can start to fight the fire you need to see where the flames are coming from. Then you will check that everyone is safe.

This is the house that has a fire. You speak to the other firefighters to agree on how to tackle the blaze.

1 Name the shapes of these:

A roof

B door

C top windows

D window to the left of the door

E window to the right of the door

Everybody is safely out of the building. But wait! You hear a barking sound – Rusty the dog is trapped upstairs. You quickly get out your ladder again. You're going to rescue him! You take:

2 minutes up the ladder

3 minutes in the house

1 minute to lift Rusty up

2 minutes to take Rusty to safety

2 How long does it take to rescue Rusty?

3 That dog is heavy! After the rescue you put Rusty on some scales to see how much he weighs. How heavy is he?

4 Of course, people weigh much more than dogs. You once carried a woman from a burning building. She weighed as much as 3 Rustys! How heavy was she?

Your gloves have an inside layer that protect your hands from heat.

5 This is the back of one of your gloves. Is it for your right or left hand?

A fire grows quickly. It can double in size every minute.

There is no one in the building, so you can now concentrate on putting out the flames. You use lots of water pumped through your hoses. You point the hose at the bottom of the fire rather than the flames. The fire is soon out.

1 Your red hoses are 15 metres long. Your black hoses are 30 metres long. You can fix them together to make a longer hose. How many of each would you use to make a hose that was 45 metres long?

2 How would you make a hose that was 90 metres long? Use the fewest number of hoses.

In an emergency, firefighters take water from nearby ponds.

3 Firefighters can choose the width of the hose as well as its length. This is the smallest hose. Use a ruler to measure it. How wide is the hose?

4 Bigger hoses are used to pump more water on to the fire. One is 6 centimetres across and another is 9 centimetres across. Look at this number line. Which letter marks the number 6?

5 What number does the letter E mark?

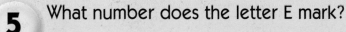

Firefighters can control the amount of water flowing through the hose and the pattern of the spray.

The fire is out, but is it safe to go back into the building? You and your team check that there is no chance of another fire starting. You also check that the building is safe for people to go into it.

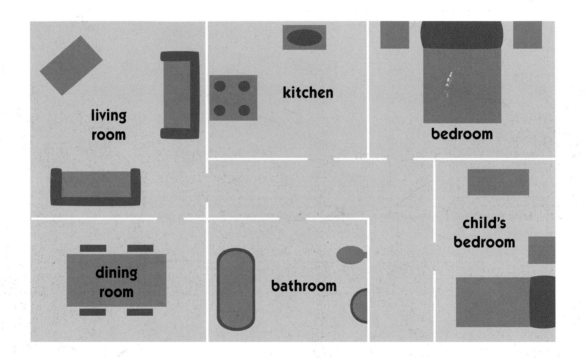

living room

kitchen

bedroom

dining room

bathroom

child's bedroom

1 This is a plan of the house. You check the fire is out in every room. How many rooms do you check?

2 You check the kitchen, living room, dining room and then the bathroom. Are you going clockwise or anti-clockwise?

3 How many rooms in this house are bedrooms?

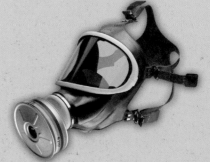

22

After the fire there are lots of burnt things to be thrown away. You help out and fill these things with rubbish:

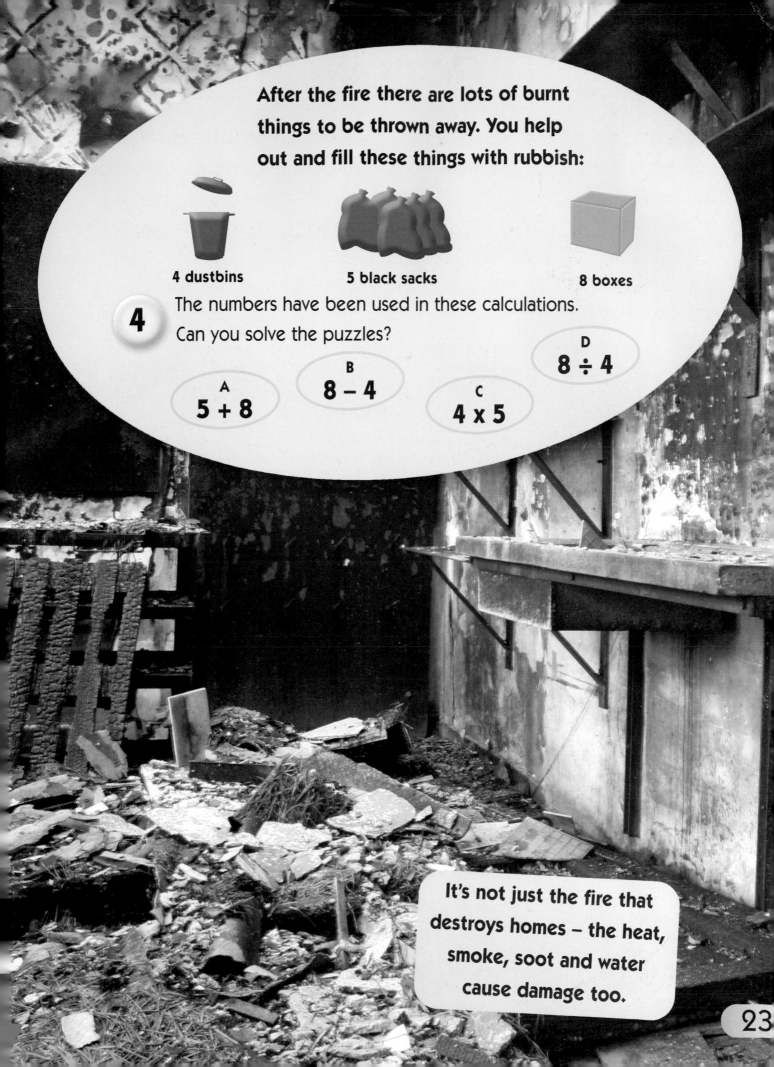

4 dustbins

5 black sacks

8 boxes

4 The numbers have been used in these calculations. Can you solve the puzzles?

A 5 + 8

B 8 − 4

C 4 x 5

D 8 ÷ 4

It's not just the fire that destroys homes – the heat, smoke, soot and water cause damage too.

After W--rk – Staying Fit

Firefighters need to be fit and strong. They have to bend, stretch, lift and carry each day in their job. After work you do more exercise to make sure you can tackle any danger.

1 You have hand weights to lift. You would like a new set. You want a set that costs less than £17, and is not heavier than 4½ kilograms. Which set is best?

	Cost	Weight
Set 1	£10	5 kg
Set 2	£20	4½ kg
Set 3	£15	4 kg
Set 4	£16	5½ kg

Using a treadmill is one way firefighters keep fit.

2 You have a skipping rope and count your skips. You do 35 skips and then you do 34. How many in total?

When you exercise, your heart pumps your blood around your body quicker. You can check your pulse to find out how fast your heart is pumping.

3 Before you start skipping your heart rate is 75 beats per minute. Afterwards, its gone up to 92 beats per minute. How many beats has it gone up by?

4 You end your fitness time lying on your mat to relax. Are these sentences true or false?

A The mat is more than half a metre wide

B The mat is 1 metre long

C The width is half of the length

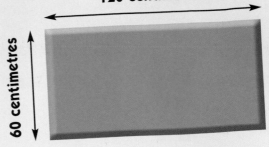

120 centimetres

60 centimetres

Firefighters must be fit. The uniform and equipment weighs about 36 kilograms – and that's before they have to rescue anybody!

In the News

Big fires are reported in the local newspaper. Your firefighting team is often mentioned. You talk to the reporters about what started the fire, how many people were rescued and how you put the fire out.

YOUR LOCAL NEWS

Every Wednesday & Saturday

50p

People rescued from fire!

A brave firefighter rescued five people trapped in a burning building yesterday. The building on York Road caught on fire at seven o'clock last night. Nine firefighters tackled the blaze. They took one hour and eighteen minutes to put the fire out. The people trapped in the building were led to safety by firefighter Angie Jones. Angie, aged twenty six, has been a firefighter for three years. Angie loves her job, and has put out forty eight fires so far.

The fire started at 20 York Road. Two other buildings were also damaged by the fire.

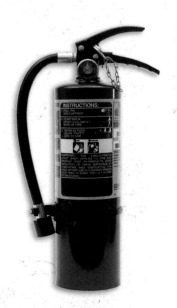

1 How much does the newspaper cost?

2 How many times a week does the paper come out?

3 How old was Angie when she first became a firefighter?

4 What is the house number of the building where the fire started?

Look at the newspaper report. All of the numbers have been written as words. Can you answer these questions, giving your answer in figures?

5 How many firefighters tackled the blaze?

6 How old is Angie?

7 How long did it take the firefighters to put the fire out?

8 How many fires has Angie put out?

Firefighting is dangerous. Angie carries an alarm that will beep loudly if she becomes unconscious.

St ying S fe

Firefighters know what to do if they see a fire.
Do you? If you see a fire you should not try to put
it out. Instead you need to raise the alarm.
Shout "Fire! Fire!" very loudly, and get out of the
building as quickly as you can. Then tell an adult, or dial 999.

HOW DID IT START?

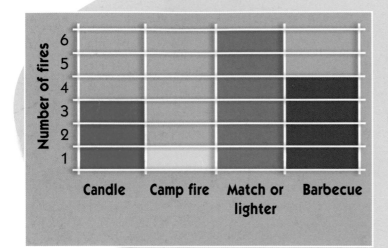

This block graph shows
how some fires started.

1 How many fires were caused by a match or lighter?

2 What is the total number of camp fire and barbecue fires?

3 What caused the fewest fires?

A   **B**   **C**   **D**

4 To stay safe we must read signs and understand what they mean.
What shape are these signs?

A – danger!

B – read safety instructions below this sign

C – fire extinguisher

D – follow arrow to find fire exit

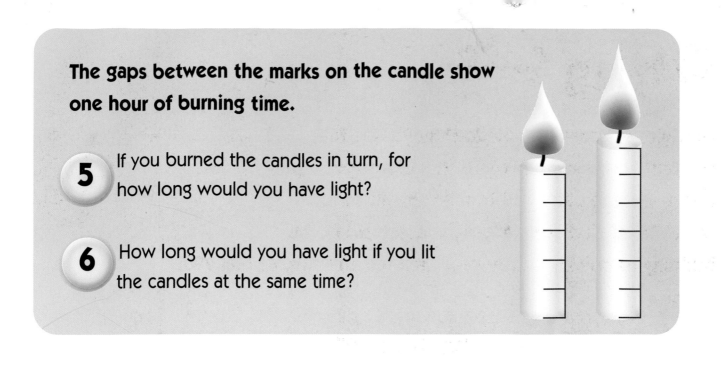

The gaps between the marks on the candle show one hour of burning time.

5 If you burned the candles in turn, for how long would you have light?

6 How long would you have light if you lit the candles at the same time?

Enjoy fires safely. Remember, firefighters are happiest when there are no fires for them to put out!

Tips and Help

PAGES 6-7

Sharing and grouping – When we break up a number into equal groups, each group is a fraction of the whole number. Here each group is a team of firefighters.

Block graph – A block graph is a kind of chart where we can compare two kinds of information. In this block graph one 'block' means one fire and the graph compares numbers of kinds of fire.

PAGES 8-9

Telling the time – When the shorter hand (or hour hand) is halfway between numbers on the clock, and the longer hand (or minute hand) has gone halfway around the clock (when it is pointing to the six) we say the time is 'half past'.

Difference – Finding the difference is the same as subtracting. The difference between the numbers of helmets and jackets can be written as 18 – 14. Remember, in these subtractions we put the larger number first.

PAGES 10-11

Groups of two – When working with groups of two it helps to learn the pattern of counting in twos like this:
Zero 2 4 6 8 10 12 14 16 18 20 22 24

Following a map – It can help to follow a map if you turn the map to match the direction you are going. Turn the book around if you need to, so that the road is facing the way you want to go.

PAGES 12-13

Half – The symbol for half is ½ which shows a '1', a line meaning 'shared by' and '2'. (One shared by two is a half).

PAGES 14-15

Compass points – N, S, E and W (North, South, East and West) are called the points of the compass. A compass shows which direction is north. It can help us find our way and talk about direction.

Pictogram – A chart where a picture is used to show one or more than one things. In this pictogram a flame picture means one fire.

PAGES 16-17

Number line – The ladder here is like a number line. It is as though there is a number on each rung. You can use the number line to count on and back (or up and down the ladder).

PAGES 18-19

Naming shapes – To help name flat shapes look at their sides and corners:

Square four sides all the same length and four right angle corners

Rectangle two pairs of sides the same in length and four right angle corners

Triangle three sides

Circle every point on a circle is the same distance from its centre.

Scales and dials – In maths these help us 'read off' measures. We need to look very carefully to check that the measure is correct. For example these scales show us kilograms.

PAGES 24-25

Reading a Table – When we collect information and write it in lists we call this a table. Here the lists are side by side, so that we can compare them. In this table you can compare the four sets of hand weights.

Metre – There are 100 centimetres in 1 metre.

PAGES 20-21

Measuring with a ruler – Be careful to place the ruler so that the '0' (zero) is exactly on one end of the line to be measured. Then you can 'read off' the width of the hose at the other end of the line.

PAGES 26-27

Words for numbers – Remember numbers can be written in words like 'one, two, three'… and figures or symbols. We use just ten symbols to write all numbers. The symbols are 0 1 2 3 4 5 6 7 8 9. Where we put each symbol shows its value. So the one in the number 123 is one hundred, in 12 it is one ten and in 31 it is one one.

PAGES 22-23

Clockwise – Clockwise is the direction the hands of a clock move around.

Anti-clockwise – Anti-clockwise is the other way around.

PAGES 28-29

Signs – It is important to be able to read signs. Spot them in buildings, in the street and in your home. They are often warnings. Look also at their shapes as kinds of sign are often the same in shape.

Answers

PAGES 6-7

1	8 people	**4**	4 fires
2	30 fires	**5**	15 fires
3	75 fires		

PAGES 8-9

1	3 days	**5**	lunch
2	8:30 am	**6**	2 hours
3	checking the engine	**7**	4
4	training	**8**	18

PAGES 10-11

1	A and E	**3**	6 minutes
2	10	**4**	C

PAGES 12-13

1	6 vehicles	**5**	tree
2	4 kilometres	**6**	12
3	90 times	**7**	camp fire
4	fire engine		

PAGES 14-15

1	no	**4**	9 fires
2	yes	**5**	11 trees
3	camp fire		

PAGES 16-17

1	3 metres	**4**	120 litres
2	Rung 2	**5**	9 hoses
3	Rung 8		

PAGES 18-19

1	A triangle	**2**	8 minutes
	B rectangle	**3**	20 kilograms
	C rectangles	**4**	60 kilograms
	D square	**5**	right hand
	E circle		

PAGES 20-21

1	1 black hose and 1 red hose, or 3 red hoses	**3**	5 centimetres
		4	D
2	3 black houses	**5**	9

PAGES 22-23

1	6 rooms	**4**	A =13
2	anti-clockwise		B = 4
3	2		C = 20
			D = 2

PAGES 24-25

1	Set 3	**4**	A true
2	69 jumps		B false
3	17 beats per minute		C true

PAGES 26-27

1	50p	**6**	26
2	twice a week	**7**	1 hour and 18 minutes
3	23		
4	20	**8**	48
5	9 firefighters		

PAGES 28-29

1	6 fires		C square
2	5 fires		D rectangle
3	camp fire	**5**	11 hours
4	A triangle	**6**	6 hours
	B circle		